PHILIPPINES

By Theia Lake and
Joanne Mattern

Published in 2025 by Cavendish Square Publishing, LLC
2544 Clinton Street, Buffalo, NY 14224

Second Edition

Website: cavendishsq.com

Library of Congress Cataloging-in-Publication Data

Names: Lake, Theia, author. | Mattern, Joanne, author.
Title: Philippines / Theia Lake and Joanne Mattern.
Description: Second edition. | Buffalo : Cavendish Square Publishing, [2025] | Series: Exploring world cultures | Includes index.
Identifiers: LCCN 2024008651 (print) | LCCN 2024008652 (ebook) | ISBN 9781502670922 (library binding) | ISBN 9781502670915 (paperback) | ISBN 9781502670939 (ebook)
Classification: LCC DS655 .L25 2025 (print) | LCC DS655 (ebook) | DDC 959.9--dc23/eng/20240307
LC record available at https://lccn.loc.gov/2024008651
LC ebook record available at https://lccn.loc.gov/2024008652

Writers: Joanne Mattern; Theia Lake (second edition)
Editor: Theresa Emminizer
Copyeditor: Danielle Haynes
Designer: Andrea Davison-Bartolotta

The photographs in this book are used by permission and through the courtesy of: Cover Elena Yakusheva/Shutterstock.com; p. 4 Perfect Lazybones/Shutterstock.com; p. 5 hijodeponggol/Shutterstock.com; p. 6 Rainer Lesniewski/Shutterstock.com; p. 7 Igor Plotnikov/Shutterstock.com; p. 9 (main) Lano Lan/Shutterstock.com; p. 9 (inset) File:Philippine Independence, July 4 1946.jpg/Wikimedia Commons; p. 10 Offcial White House Photo by Cameron Smith; p. 11 Walter Eric Sy/Shutterstock.com; p. 12 mayura benjarattanapakee/Shutterstock.com; p. 13 Phuong D. Nguyen/Shutterstock.com; p. 15 (top) Stephane Bidouze/Shutterstock.com; p. 15 (bottom) Thierry Eidenweil/Shutterstock.com; pp. 16, 24 Kobby Dagan/Shutterstock.com; pp. 17, 21 Tony Magdaraog/Shutterstock.com; p. 18 File:Bayanihan 2.JPG/Wikimedia Commons; p. 19 Sun_Shine/Shutterstock.com; p. 20 Richie Chan/Shutterstock.com; p. 22 Linaimages/Shutterstock.com; p. 23 Aldwin Joseph Gimena/Shutterstock.com; p. 25 MDV Edwards/Shutterstock.com; p. 26 Oscar Espinosa/Shutterstock.com; p. 27 Davdeka/Shutterstock.com; p. 28 Brent Hofacker/Shutterstock.com; p. 29 junpinzon/Shutterstock.com.

CPSIA compliance information: Batch #CS25CSQ: For further information contact Cavendish Square Publishing LLC at 1-877-980-4450.

Printed in the United States of America

CONTENTS

INTRODUCTION

The Philippines is an island country in the Pacific Ocean. People who live there are called Filipinos. Manila is the capital city of this Southeast Asian nation. It's one of the most crowded cities in the world!

The Philippines was named after Philip II, who was the king of Spain from 1556 to 1598. The Spanish colonized the Philippines during the 1500s. The United States later took control of the country. The Philippines became independent in 1946.

Filipinos cut ***terraces*** *into the lower parts of mountains. These terraces are used for farming rice.*

The Philippines is home to many rare, or uncommon, plants and animals. It's a country of mountains, volcanoes, and sandy beaches. The Filipino people have a long, rich **heritage** that's been shaped by the country's unique, or one-of-kind, geography. The culture—the beliefs and way of life—of Filipino people is very **diverse**. The Filipino people come from many **ethnic** backgrounds and speak many different languages.

Filipinos wear colorful masks at a festival, or gathering, in Bacolod.

GEOGRAPHY

The Philippines is an archipelago, or group of islands. The Philippines has more than 7,000 islands and islets (small islands)! Many of these islands and islets don't even have names. They spread out in the shape of a triangle and are surrounded by the Philippine Sea, the Celebes Sea, the Sulu Sea, and the South China Sea.

This is a map of the Philippines.

FACT!

The Philippine archipelago is 1,150 miles (1,851 kilometers) long from north to south.

The Philippine islands have beautiful coastal views.

The Philippine islands fall into three main groups: Luzon, the Visayas, and Mindanao. The Luzon group includes the Luzon, Mindoro, and Palawan islands in the northern part of the Philippines. The Visayas group is in the middle. It includes Bohol, Cebu, Leyte, Masbate, Negros, Panay, and Samar. Mindanao is in the south.

MIGHTY MOUNTAINS

Most of the Philippine islands have high mountains. The Sierra Madre is the longest mountain range in the Philippines. The two highest mountains are on Mindanao Island. Mount Apo is 9,692 feet (2,954 meters). Mount Dulang-Dulang is 9,649 feet (2,941 m).

HISTORY

The first settlers came to the Philippines from other parts of Asia thousands of years ago. After the 900s CE, Filipinos began to trade with China.

Then, in 1521, Ferdinand Magellan arrived in the Philippines from Spain. In 1565, more Spanish people settled on the islands. Spain ruled the Philippines until 1898. In August 1898, the United States took control.

In 1946, the Philippines became independent. Between 1965 and 1986, the islands were ruled by a harsh leader named Ferdinand Marcos. Then, a revolution put President Corazon Aquino in power. She brought **democratic** rule back to the Philippines.

THE PHILIPPINE-AMERICAN WAR

The United States took control of the Philippines at the end of the Spanish-American War in 1898. However, Filipinos wanted to fight for independence! On February 4, 1899, American soldiers opened fire on Filipinos in Manila, beginning the Philippine-American War, which lasted until 1902.

This photo shows the American flag being lowered while the Philippine flag is raised during an independence celebration on July 4, 1946.

FACT!

Filipinos fought against Spanish rule for many years before the Spanish-American War. They helped the U.S. fight Spain hoping to gain independence.

The Heritage of Cebu monument, pictured here, shows important events in Philippines history.

GOVERNMENT

Today, the Philippines is a presidential **republic**. This means its government has three branches: executive, legislative, and judicial.

The president leads the executive branch. He or she is elected every six years. The president chooses advisers, or helpers, to be in their cabinet. Each cabinet member runs a part of the government.

FACT!

The national anthem, or song, of the Philippines is called "Lupang Hinirang," which means "Chosen Land."

Ferdinand "Bongbong" Marcos Jr. became the 17th president of the Philippines in 2022.

The legislative branch makes the laws. It's called the Congress of the Philippines. The judicial branch is made up of the Supreme Court.

The **Constitution** of the Philippines was ratified, or made official, in 1987.

PROVINCES

The Philippines has 82 provinces, which are similar to U.S. states. Each province in the Philippines has its own local government of elected officials. The governor is the leader, and a legislature makes laws for the province.

The Philippine flag pictures a golden sun and three gold stars, which stand for the three main island groups.

THE ECONOMY

The Philippines has one of the strongest **economies** in Southeast Asia. In the past, **agriculture** made up most of the nation's economy. Today, about one-third of Filipinos work in agriculture. Rice and corn are the most popular foods to grow. The Philippines also sends sugar and coconuts to other parts of the world.

FACT!

Many tasty tropical fruits are grown in the Philippines, including pineapples, mangoes, and papayas.

Philippine currency, or money, is called pesos.

Transportation is also an important field. Few Filipinos own cars. Instead, they use public buses and trains. Boats called ferries carry people from island to island.

People also work in stores, hotels, banks, restaurants, and businesses. Others are teachers, doctors, and government workers.

TOURISM

Tourism, or travel, is an important part of the economy. People from all over the world travel to the Philippines to see its beautiful beaches. The Philippines has one of the longest coastlines in the world.

People are out shopping on a busy street in Manila.

THE ENVIRONMENT

The environment, or natural surroundings, of the Philippines is beautiful and rich with life. The rainforests are filled with giant fig trees and lauan trees, and a vine called rattan. Mangrove trees grow by the coast. These trees have long roots that rise out of the water.

Many different animals live in the Philippines. Some, such as the water buffalo, are very large. Others, such as the tarsier (a monkey-like animal), are small. Many of the animals that live in the Philippines can't be found anywhere else in the world!

NATIONAL PARKS

There are 35 national parks in the Philippines. The plants and animals in these areas are protected, or kept safe, by law. Puerto Princesa Subterranean River National Park is home to an underground river that winds through beautiful caves.

The Philippine eagle is the country's national bird. It's one of the rarest birds in the world.

FACT!

The waters around the Philippines are filled with life! Sharks, eels, lionfish, dolphins, and starfish all live there.

Whale sharks are the biggest fish in the world! Tourists come to the Philippines to swim with them.

THE PEOPLE TODAY

There are about 118 million people living in the Philippines today. Most Filipinos are of Malay descent, meaning their **ancestors** came from the area around the Malay **Peninsula**. Some also have Chinese, Spanish, and American backgrounds.

FACT!

The Filipino ethnic groups have been heavily influenced, or shaped, by the Spanish and American presence in their country.

A young Filipino girl holds up a star in a market in Manila.

Filipino dancers dress in **traditional** clothing at a festival.

Filipinos belong to many different ethnic groups. The Tagalogs and the Cebuanos are two large groups. Most Tagalogs live in or around Manila. Cebuanos live in the middle of the country. Other ethnic groups in the Philippines include Bisaya/Binisay people and Ilocano people. There are many cultural differences among the many ethnic groups in the Philippines.

NAMES

Many Filipinos have Spanish names. That's because when the Spanish ruled the Philippines, they made Filipinos use Spanish last names. Today, many people go by names that are common in the United States and Spain. Some Filipinos use traditional Tagalog names.

LIFESTYLE

The family is the center of life in the Philippines. Many families live in cities. Philippine cities are very crowded and noisy. People who live there live in apartments or small houses.

Some Filipinos live in villages in the country or along the coast. Country homes are often made of wood and leaves. Houses near the water are built on tall poles so they will stay dry.

Moving houses is just one part of the larger idea and spirit of Bayanihan.

Bayanihan is an important part of Filipino culture. It's a spirit of community and helping one another. Part of Bayanihan is the tradition of neighbors helping one another move their houses.

FACT!

Religion, or faith, is an important part of life in the Philippines.

These children are walking to school on Palawan Island.

EDUCATION

Children must go to elementary school from ages 7 to 13. After elementary school, many teenagers go to a secondary school for 4 years. Most Filipinos go to college after that. Some begin work instead.

RELIGION

The Roman Catholic religion was a big part of Spanish colonization in the Philippines. **Missionaries** taught the religion to the Native people. Today, more than 80 percent of Filipinos are still Catholic. They celebrate, or observe, traditional Catholic holidays, including Christmas, Easter, and the feast days of different saints.

FACT!

Animism, or the belief that trees and plants have spirits, is an important part of Indigenous, or Native, beliefs.

The Manila Cathedral is a large Catholic church in the capital city.

Some Filipinos practice other forms of Christianity. The Philippine Independent Church is the most popular. It was started in 1902. Some Filipinos practice a mix of Christian and ancient, or very old, beliefs.

During the Catholic feast of the Black Nazarene, believers walk barefoot through Manila.

OTHER RELIGIONS

About 5 percent of Filipinos are Muslim. They belong to a collection of ethnic groups called the Moro people. A small number of Filipinos are Hindus, Buddhists, or Baha'is.

LANGUAGE

Filipino is the official language of the Philippines. Filipino is based on the Tagalog language. However, people in different parts of the country speak different languages. There are more than 100 languages spoken in the Philippines! They include Tagalog, Cebuano, Ilocano, Bicol, and Samarnon.

Kamusta ka? means "How are you?" in Filipino.

Students learn Filipino and English in school. English is used in business and the government. Classes at universities are usually taught in English. In the past, Filipino students had to learn Spanish in school. Spanish is still widely spoken there.

WORDS TO KNOW

Here are some key words in the Filipino language. *Oo* means yes. *Hindi* means no. *Salamat* means thank you! *Paalam* means goodbye. *Magandang umaga*, *magandang hapon*, and *magandang gabi* mean good morning, good afternoon, and good evening.

FACT!

Po is a Filipino word. It can be used in the middle or at the end of most sentences to show respect or be polite, especially to someone older than you.

The signs in this Philippines classroom are in English.

ARTS AND FESTIVALS

The Philippines has many fun and colorful festivals. Some celebrate Catholic saints and traditions. Others celebrate folk traditions, art, and dancing.

Traditional crafts include weaving, or cloth-making, woodworking, and basket making. People in Cebu create beautiful art out of shells.

The Sinulog Festival in Cebu honors religion and culture.

FACT!

Painting religious figures or scenes was very popular during the time that the Spanish ruled the Philippines. Later, painters showed Native people in traditional clothes.

Music is a very important part of Filipino life. People enjoy many kinds of music, including rock and jazz. Many people attend concerts or play music at home. Some Filipinos enjoy dancing. The Tinikling is the national dance of the Philippines. It involves dancing with bamboo poles.

LITERATURE

The literature, or writing, of the Philippines includes themes, or ideas, of freedom. Literature was one of the ways the people called for independence from Spain and, later, the United States.

These two women are doing the Tinikling dance.

FUN AND PLAY

Basketball is a popular sport in the Philippines. Many children enjoy playing basketball on public courts or in school. Other popular sports include golf, tennis, boxing, and volleyball.

FACT!

Arnis is a kind of martial art that's practiced in the Philippines. It involves skillful movements of self-defense, or protection, with sticks.

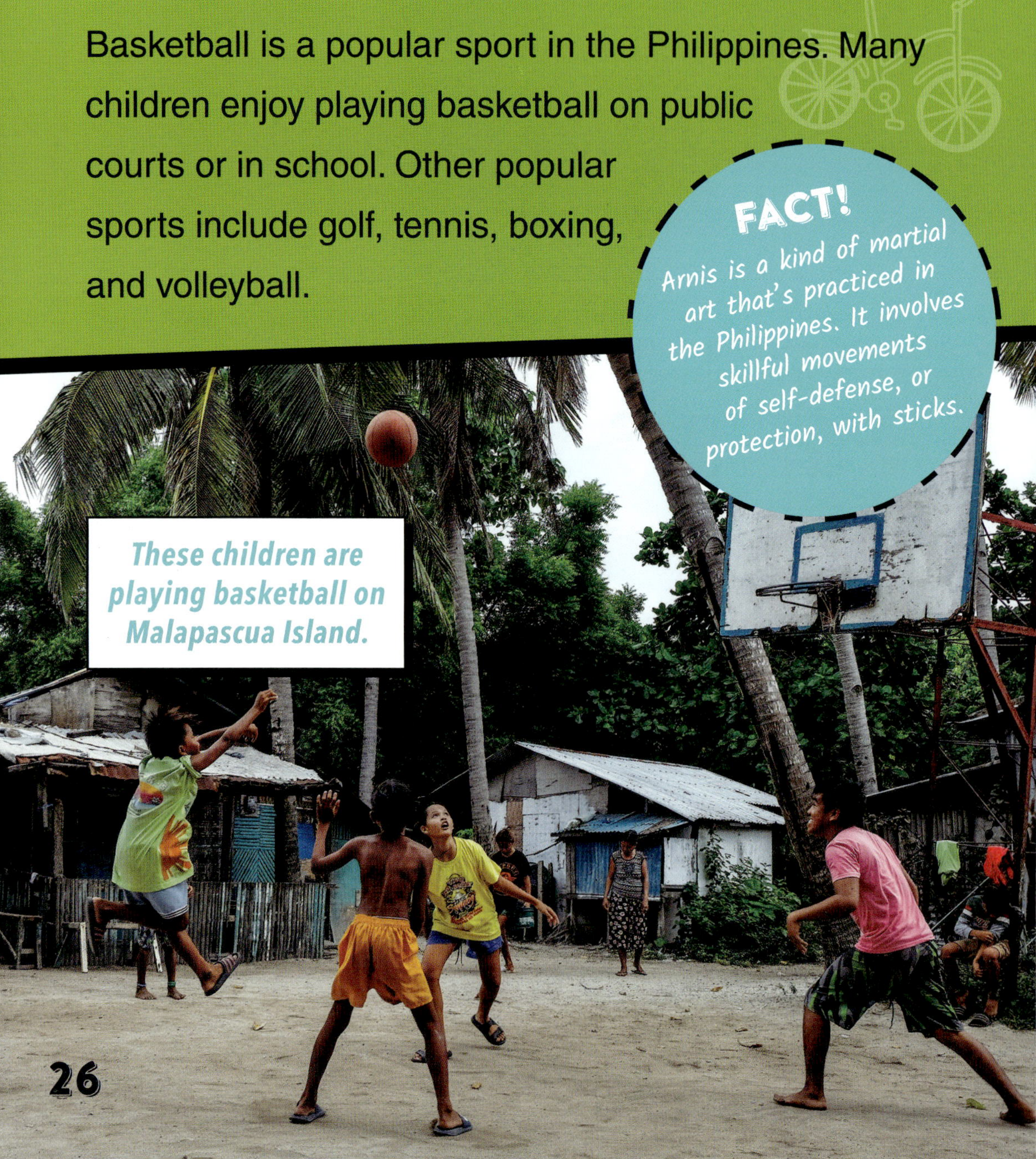

These children are playing basketball on Malapascua Island.

Jai alai is another popular sport. Players tie a small scoop to their arm. One player throws a ball against a wall using the scoop. Then, an opposing player must catch it and throw it back.

The Philippine Women's National Football (soccer) team, called the Filipinas, played in the FIFA World Cup for the first time in 2023.

SIPA

Sipa is a traditional sport in the Philippines. It's somewhat like volleyball, but players can only hit the ball over the net with their knees and feet. Many Filipinos think of sipa as their national sport because it dates back to before the time of Spanish colonization.

This player is playing sipa, which is like kick volleyball.

FOOD

Filipino cuisine, or cooking, is filled with tasty flavors. Meat is a big part of meals. Rice is also very important. It can be boiled or fried. Sometimes it's baked into cakes. Children enjoy a drink made of rice mixed with hot chocolate!

FACT!
Kain na! means "Let's eat!" in Tagalog.

Adobo is widely thought of as the national dish of the Philippines.

Adobo is a popular Filipino dish. Adobo is a sauce made of vinegar, soy sauce, and garlic. It's served over chicken, pork, beef, or vegetables.

Kare-kare is another special Filipino dish. It's a stew made with oxtail and peanuts.

LECHON

Lechon is a special meal in the Philippines, somewhat like a barbeque. It involves slowly roasting a whole pig over an open fire. This often takes many hours! Lechon is famous for its crispy skin and tender, or soft, meat.

Halo halo is a Filipino dessert made with crushed ice, jam, jackfruit, and more!

GLOSSARY

agriculture: Farming.

ancestor: A person from whom one is descended, or related to.

constitution: The basic laws by which a country, state, or group is governed.

diverse: Varied and different.

democratic: Relating to a system of government in which the people elect, or choose, their leaders.

economy: The way in which goods and services are made, sold, and used in a country or area.

ethnic: Of or relating to large groups of people who have the same cultural background and ways of life.

heritage: The traditions and beliefs that are part of the history of a group or nation.

missionary: Someone who travels to a new place to spread their faith.

peninsula: An area of land almost entirely surrounded by water.

republic: A country governed by elected representatives and an elected leader.

terrace: A flat area cut into a hill or slope.

traditional: Relating to something that's been used or done by people in a particular society for a long time.

FIND OUT MORE

Books

Bird, Thomas. *Insight Guides: The Philippines*. London, UK: Apa Publications, 2023.

Harding, Paul, Greg Bloom, Celeste Brash, Michael Grosberg, and Iain Stewart. *Lonely Planet Philippines*. Oakland, CA: Lonely Planet Publishing, 2022.

Morton, Owen, and Thomas Bird. *The Rough Guide to the Philippines*. London, UK: Apa Publications, 2023.

Websites

Department of Tourism: Philippines
www.philippines.travel/
Discover all there is to see and do in the Philippines.

***National Geographic Kids*: Philippines**
www.kids.nationalgeographic.com/geography/countries/article/philippines
Learn more about the history, people, and environment of the Philippines.

Video

Wake Up in the Philippines
www.youtu.be/Pmf7YVK5Bus
See some of what makes the Philippines so special to visit.

Publisher's note to educators and parents: Our editors have carefully reviewed these websites to ensure that they are suitable for students. Many websites change frequently, however, and we cannot guarantee that a site's future contents will continue to meet our high standards of quality and educational value. Be advised that students should be closely supervised whenever they access the internet.

INDEX